To: _____

From: _____

golf
on the
WiLD
side

SOURCEBOOKS, INC.
NAPERVILLE, ILLINOIS

Published by Sourcebooks, Inc.
P.O. Box 4410, Naperville, Illinois 60567-4410
(630) 961-3900
FAX: (630) 961-2168
www.sourcebooks.com

Library of Congress Cataloging-in-Publication Data

Golf on the wild side / by Sourcebooks, Inc.
    p. cm.
 ISBN 1-40220-091-9 (alk. paper)
 1. Golf—Humor. I. Sourcebooks, Inc.
PN6231.G68 G65 2004
818'.602—dc22

                              2003020088

Printed and bound in the United States of America
LB 10 9 8 7 6 5 4 3 2 1

"If you think it's hard to meet new people, try picking up the wrong golf ball."

—Jack Lemmon

"The older you get the stronger the wind gets—and it's always in your face."

–Jack Nicklaus

There's eighteen holes out there just waiting for you. Toss the clubs in the trunk, call up your golfing buddies, and haul out to the links. The next four (OK, five) hours are all yours. Pull out the big dog, then grip it and rip it. Play a wood in the rough and tear it to the green. Trash talk your foursome while you try a forty-footer...blindfolded. No fairway is too narrow, no trap too deep if you're having a blast. Golf is a sport, play hard.

As soon as you get to the course, you generously spring for carts, and you even choose a forecaddy for the group. Your new caddy for the round is a stringy high school kid named Walter, who somehow seems quite wise for his young age. And the way he meditates as he waits for you to begin is actually quite calming.

"When I'm on a golf course and it starts to rain and lightning, I hold up my one iron, 'cause I know even God can't hit a one iron."

—Lee Trevino

"Ninety percent of putts that are short don't go in."

—Yogi Berra

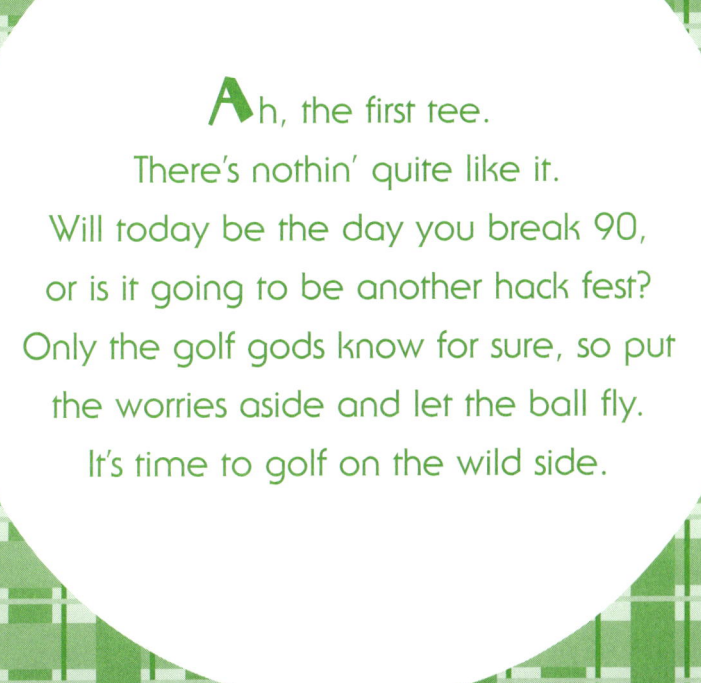

Ah, the first tee.
There's nothin' quite like it.
Will today be the day you break 90,
or is it going to be another hack fest?
Only the golf gods know for sure, so put
the worries aside and let the ball fly.
It's time to golf on the wild side.

Now you're rollin'! You smashed the first drive 250 down the center of the fairway. You humbly accept the congrats of your foursome (hoping they didn't notice that your third "practice" swing was actually a missed shot). It may or may not be the only shot you'll hit all day, but for now it doesn't matter: you're sitting pretty.

"Always throw your clubs ahead of you.
That way you don't have to waste
energy going back to pick them up."

—Tommy Bolt

"Gimme: An agreement between two losers who can't putt."

–Jim Bishop

And of course, as must follow every good shot, you're now lying 4 just off the green after shanking your second shot into the woods, then using two strokes to force your way out of the Amazonian tangle they smugly refer to as "Open rough." Sigh. You give it a short chip to try and get it close, and it starts rolling… rolling…rolling…hits the pin and in! You try not to look smug. What a shot!

Three holes in and the round is starting off well. But now comes the real test: a 180-yard par 3, water on the left, sand on the right. They call it the Widowmaker. Only the best shot can hit this dance floor. But with the wind behind you and your trusty 5 iron at your side, you're feeling like today might just be your lucky day.

"GOLF is a game in which you yell 'fore,' shoot six, and write down five."

—Paul Harvey

"Golf is like a grindstone: whether it grinds you down or polishes you up depends on what you're made of."

—English saying

No such luck. You're buried in the desert behind a lip so big it's like you're shooting into a brick wall. There's only one thing you can do: swing hard and swing deep. With a blast, you send up a Sahara-class sandstorm that makes your foursome duck for cover while your ball lands just on the green. Not perfect, but now you're putting for par!

After an ordeal like that, you deserve a cold drink. The beverage cart is nowhere in sight, but that's okay; you came prepared. After a few nights spent rigging it up with some freeze packs and a couple of thermos liners, your golf bag doubles as a portable cooler. It fits eighteen cans (and two bags of chips), so you even have enough to share with your friends.

Walter politely declines.

"They say that life is a lot like golf—
don't believe them.
Golf is a lot more complicated."

—Gardner Dickinson

"Golf is the worst drug in the world. You just keep coming back for more embarrassment."

–Deacon Jones

The dreaded par 5 looms ahead: five hundred yards, two doglegs, and a green that laughs down at you from atop a small hill. The par 5s are make-or-break. Get it to the green quickly and you're primed for a bird. Duff a shot and you've got a long way to go. Time to get wild.

Sometimes it pays to be bold. Everyone else is playing it safe with an iron, but you know that it's driver time. With a smooth swing and just enough power, you've got the ball flying. It comes down with a nice roll, barely staying on the fairway, but fifty yards ahead of your buddies. Walter nods knowingly at your mastery of the psychological game.

"Got more dirt than ball. Here we go again."

—Alan Shepard, 1971 moon walk

"Half of golf
is fun;
the other
half is
putting."

—Peter Dobereiner

But wouldn't you know it: some lazy hacker didn't replace his divot, so now you're hitting out of a small patch of dirt. You try to zone it out, but you hit the ground early and send a screamer only a hundred yards. Well, you take the good, you take the bad….And at least your next shot makes the green.

Now it gets interesting.
You've got a thirty-footer for bird,
going right to left in the front and then
swinging back right down a ridge that puts
the Grand Canyon to shame. Your friends are
smirking behind their golf gloves, but you don't
care. You see the line and it's looking sweet.
And even though it rims around the cup
and dies an inch away, at least you
replaced those smirks with
open jaws.

"Golf's three ugliest words:
still your shot."

—Dave Marr

"What goes up must come down. But don't expect it to come down where you can find it."

–Lily Tomlin

As you approach the ninth tee, you're feeling loose and happy with your swing. You hit a clean drive that doesn't fly, but comes down straight and safe. You hop in the cart feeling good; if you par this hole you'll round out the front nine with a 45—a damn good start if you do say so yourself.

At the halfway house, you award Walter with a hot dog and a Coke for his valuable help. Walter is pleased. And as the current leader, you also get stuck buying dogs and drinks for the rest of your group. But when you're flying this high, the money doesn't matter. The sun is shining, the geese are honking, and you're ready for the home stretch.

"WHY am I usiNG a New PuTTeR? Because the LasT one DiDN'T fLoaT too weLL."

–Craig Stadler

"Happiness
is a long
walk with
a putter."

—Greg Norman

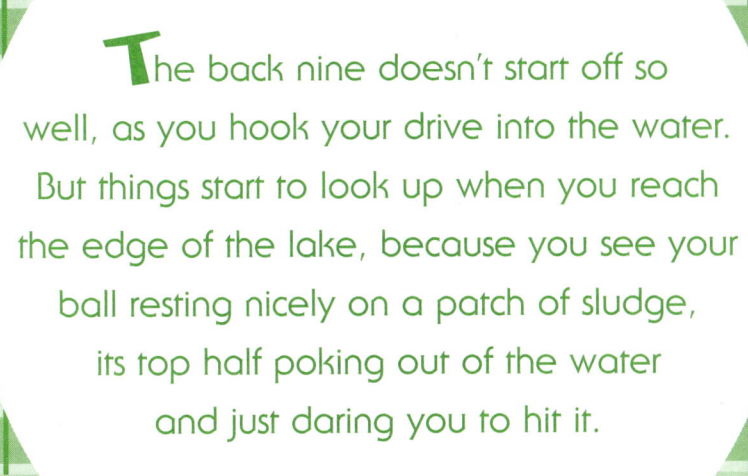

The back nine doesn't start off so well, as you hook your drive into the water. But things start to look up when you reach the edge of the lake, because you see your ball resting nicely on a patch of sludge, its top half poking out of the water and just daring you to hit it.

Your buddies think you're crazy when you announce that you're going for it. But they don't know about your secret weapon. Out of your bag you pull two garbage bags, and, with a little flair, you step a leg in each and tie the bags off above your knees. Now you're a waterproof golfing machine! Of course, the shot barely goes anywhere, but 50 yards is better than nothing.

"Have you ever noticed what golf spells backwards?"

—Al Bolska

"Golf is a game that is played on a five-inch course—the distance between your ears."

–Bobby Jones

The inexplicable law of nines has now come into play: the pace at which you play the front nine is inversely proportional to the pace at which you'll play the back nine. So, since you cruised through the front nine, you now find yourself stuck behind what seems to be the slowest foursome ever to play golf. And you can't figure out why that guy needs to waggle for three minutes when he duffs each shot anyway.

Hole 11 is a quirky little par 4. It's only 300 yards long, but the fairway shoots left on a diagonal off the tee before making an extreme dogleg back to the green. The result: a 260-yard straight shot to the green...if you're willing to try to hit it over the thickest group of oak trees this side of Oregon. You would normally hit for the fairway and try for a birdie, but today is not a normal day.

"I DON'T PLAY WELL ENOUGH TO BE ALLOWED TO THROW MY CLUBS."

—LOU HOLTZ

"I know I'm getting better at golf because I'm hitting fewer spectators."

—Gerald Ford

You rip out the driver. Your buddies try to talk you out of it, but there's no time to be afraid of trees. You put everything you've got into the swing, and hit a shot so beautiful that if it weren't for that one branch poking out of the forest canopy, you'd be on the green instead of lying one somewhere in that dark timberland.

After searching for five minutes, and interrupting a squirrel family reunion, you finally find your ball resting a foot in front of a gnarled tree. Miraculously, there's a thin line straight ahead, through which you can actually see the green. You've got a shot if you play it right. Keeping your head up and blading a 5 iron, you take the hack of all hacks and pray for the ball to stay low. Huzzah! The ball lands just short of the green.

"What other people may find
in poetry or art museums, I find
in the flight of a good drive."

—Arnold Palmer

"I'd like to see the fairways more narrow.
Then everybody would have to play
from the rough, not just me."

—Seve Ballesteros

You chip on only three feet from the cup. Your friends are signaling for a gimme, but just to make it interesting you take the putt on one foot. Sure, you're showboating, but you've it earned when the ball drops in, capping off the ugliest par ever.

The next hole is covered in geese. No one is quite sure why geese think golf courses are the most interesting places on the planet. Many golfers act the fool trying to chase them off, but you know that honey is better than vinegar. You break out the loaf of bread that you smartly bring with you on every round. Some crumbs here, some crumbs there, some crumbs in front of your opponent's ball, and watch that gaggle clear away from your shot.

"It took me seventeen years to get three thousand hits in baseball. I did it in one afternoon on the golf course."

—Hank Aaron

"I've had a good day when I don't fall out of the cart."

—Buddy Hackett

There's two holes left and you have an eighty. Hole 17 is a short par 4 with a tricky approach, and 18 is a long, uphill par 5. This means that if you par both holes, you'll be walking home with an 89. You've dreamed of breaking 90 like some men dream of walking on the moon. It's all in your hands now.

A sweet drive on 17 leaves you 135 from the hole—but this is no chip shot. The green is surrounded by sand, and the groundskeepers have craftily placed the pin all the way back today. You have to go for the stick, because to leave it short would put you behind a ridge. You make a wish and swing…

"My psychiatrist prescribed a game of golf as an antidote to the feelings of euphoria I experience from time to time."
—Bruce Lansky

"It's good sportsmanship not to pick up
lost balls while they are still rolling."

–Mark Twain

...**A**nd end up in the far trap. You somehow manage not to toss your club into the lake, and collect yourself as you approach the shot. A good shot will leave you close enough to close out the par. But you catch too much sand, and leave the ball on the fringe. Things aren't going well.

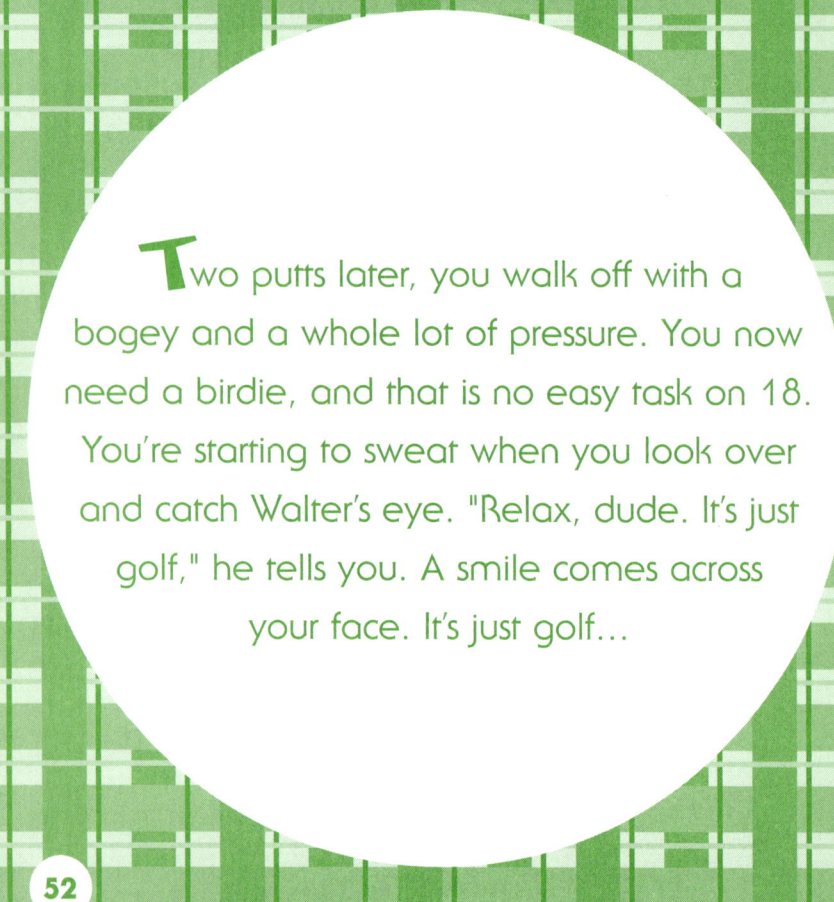

Two putts later, you walk off with a bogey and a whole lot of pressure. You now need a birdie, and that is no easy task on 18. You're starting to sweat when you look over and catch Walter's eye. "Relax, dude. It's just golf," he tells you. A smile comes across your face. It's just golf…

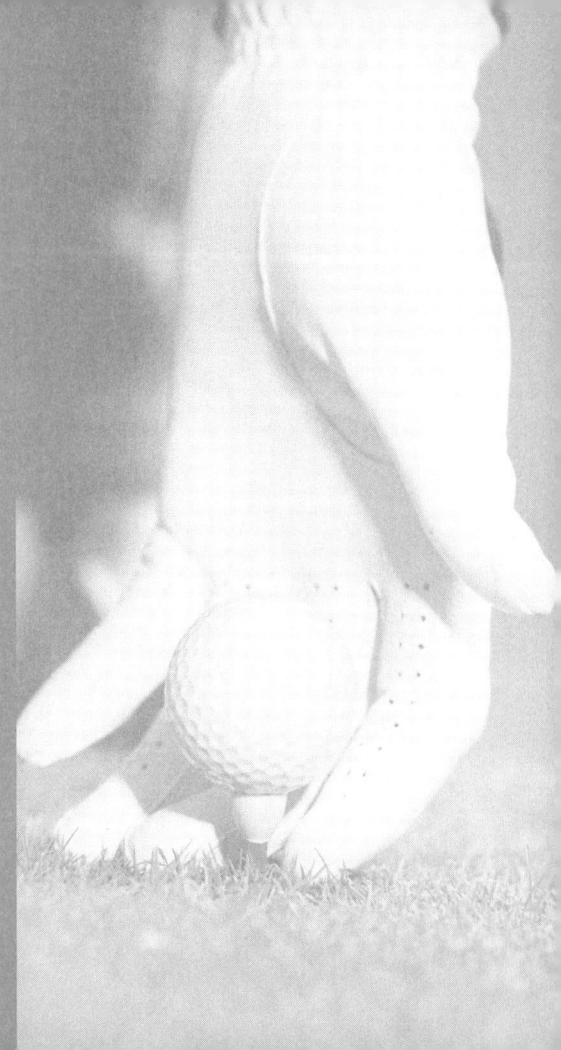

"May you
Live LONG
enough
to SHOOt
your age."

—ENGLiSH golf toast

"My best score ever is 103, but I've only been playing 15 years."

—Alex Karras

Slam! You pound your drive off the tee, sending it high and straight. It lands a nice roll, adding twenty yards to the 240 you nailed it. You step up to the second shot and blast it again, showing no mercy, and setting it down just off the green. The adrenaline is pumping, the momentum is on your side, and most of all, you're having a blast.

After a good chip, you're fifteen feet from the cup. The line breaks right to left, but not severely. It's not the hardest putt you've had all day, but with an 89 on the line, it's hard enough. You pick your spot, line it up, and pause. Your mind clears as you pull back the putter, and then glide it forward, sending the ball rolling, spinning…

"Golf is an awkward set of bodily contortions designed to produce a graceful result."

—Tommy Armour

"The more I practice,
the luckier I get."

–Gary Player

...**A**nd in! The ball drops into the cup without trepidation, and you've broken the 90 barrier. Yes! Victory at last! Your buddies are whooping it up, and rush over to clap your back and give you a high five. Even Walter is laughing, and he flashes you a little arm pump, Tiger-style.

The round is over, and as you relax with your foursome over a sandwich and drinks, you're still feeling the rush. A day on the course can sometimes make you ecstatic, and sometimes it leaves you tired and frustrated. But when you play on the wild side, ripping, flying, and tearing your way through the course, you just can't be beat.